to Her Majesty Queen Elizabeth II

Great day

© 2002 by Faber Music Ltd

5

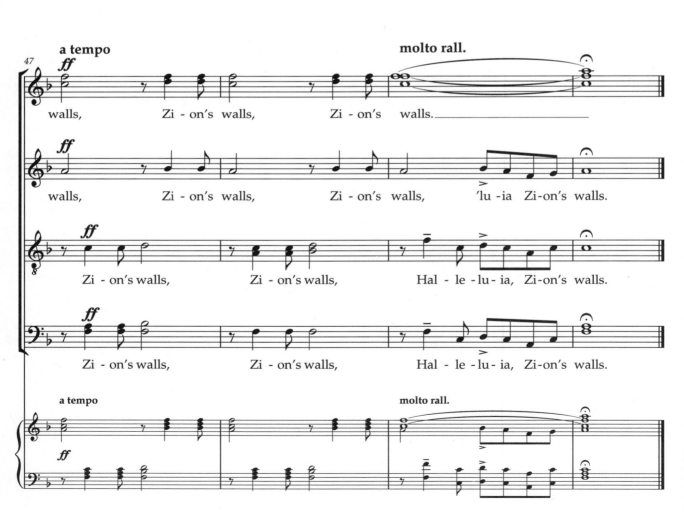

Were you there?

Traditional arr. Ken Burton

Rivers of Babylon

Traditional arr. Ken Burton

14

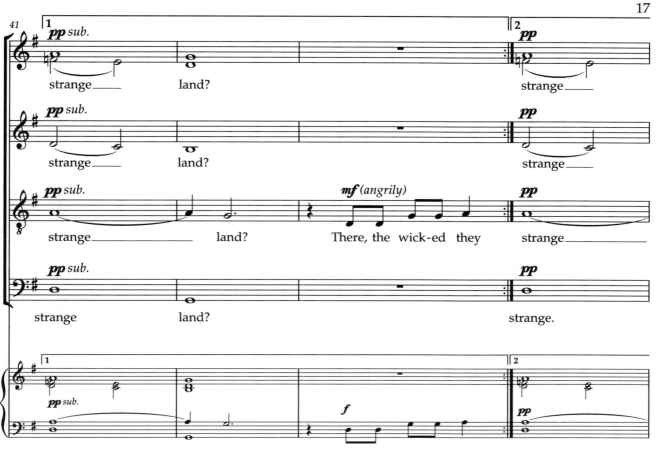

18

*audible breath, like sobbing

Deep river

Traditional arr. Ken Burton

Ready to ride

Ken Burton

Leggiero e con brio

hear the cha-riot com-ing and I'm rea-dy to ride, for I want to go to Glo-ry o - ver

Hear the cha-riot com-ing, hear the cha-riot com-ing, want to go to Glo-ry o - ver

Hear the cha-riot com-ing, hear the cha-riot com-ing, want to go to Glo-ry o - ver

Hear the cha-riot com-ing, hear the cha-riot com-ing, want to go to Glo-ry o - ver

Leggiero e con brio

(like a double bass)

on the o - ther side. I can hear the cha - riot com-ing and I'm rea - dy to ride, for I

on the o - ther side. I can hear the cha-riot com-ing, hear the cha-riot com-ing,

on the o - ther side. I can hear the cha-riot com-ing, hear the cha-riot com-ing,

on the o - ther side. I can hear the cha-riot com-ing, hear the cha-riot com-ing,

26

28

rea - dy   to ride,   for   I   want to go to Glo-ry o -ver on the o - ther side.

hear   the char-iot com-ing, want to go to Glo-ry o -ver on the o - ther side.

hear   the char-iot com-ing, want to go to Glo-ry o -ver on the o - ther side.

hear   the char-iot com-ing, want to go to Glo-ry o -ver on the o - ther side.

pp (2. *mp*) *gradually crescendo with each repeat*

Hear   the chariot coming,   hear   the chariot coming, want to go   to Glo-ry o-ver

pp (2. *mp*) *gradually crescendo with each repeat*

Hear   the chariot coming,   hear   the chariot coming, want to go to Glo-ry o-ver

pp (2. *mp*) *gradually crescendo with each repeat*

Hear   the chariot coming,   hear   the chariot coming, want to go to Glo-ry o-ver

ad lib. (swing)

ppp gradually crescendo